If Only for a Little While

Tyler Smart

BookLeaf Publishing

Presentation by *BookLeaf Publishing*

Web: www.bookleafpub.com

E-mail: info@bookleafpub.com

ISBN: 9789357615167

First edition 2022

DEDICATION

For my friends and family.

PREFACE

Men will do anything to avoid going to therapy
like writing 21 poems in 21 days.

If Only for a Little While

I've been thinking about hums lately.
A small act of taking a breath that turns into a
vibration, a vibration that turns into a sound.
Anyone can do it but it seems to be a thing
forgotten except in small tender moments of
contentment.
Used to make music out of thin air in order to
fill the cold of silence with the warmth of one's
breath.
I believe it may be the most basic but effective
expression of love.
A moment to say in pure emotion this breath I
breathe is for you.
I am living solely to be here with you in this
moment.
A moment as fleeting as a breath.
A moment that carries all that it can,
If only for a little while.

Baby Blues

I remember in Kindergarten when all the little
details of life were still new.
We all looked at each other's eyes to see what
colour they were.
Green, blue, brown, hazel, all accounted for but
with a strange hierarchy of colours.
As the rarer colours were like precious minerals
to be mined.
I don't notice eye colours much anymore,
As the most precious thing a person can have
now
Are kind eyes that make you feel seen.

Movie Night

I need to be more mindful of what's actually
being said to me.
There have been times and there will be times
when someone says something but means
something more.
I have been so focused on doing everything my
way I haven't really been listening.
When I go watch a movie whether in my room,
in my basement, or at a theatre,
My dad has always said I could watch the movie
in the living room where he spends his time.
I never understood why because I was already
seeing the movie why did it matter where I
watched it?
But I've come to realize he was asking to watch
it with me in the only way he knew how,
And I was choosing not to listen.
I am listening now.

The Ocean

Lately, I have been feeling like I am drowning.
Lost and adrift in an endless ocean,
Trying my best just to keep my head above the
water.
I always felt drawn to the water as a child,
Unwilling to leave the lake, the beach, the bath,
Every body of water was a precursor of an
argument of just five more minutes.
Somewhere over 26 years, I became terrified of
the water, or more accurately the unknown of it
all.
The mysteries of what is happening below you,
without your awareness,
Helpless against an unknown force.
I should feel scared now that I feel like I cannot
breathe and I'm thrashing with all my might,
Just to edge closer to a horizon that has no end
in sight.
And yet I feel almost at ease, almost.
Because at least I know I want to keep fighting,
that I can still breathe for the moment.
When you feel like you're drowning you can
only feel grateful for every breath you get.
And this feeling of being lost at sea might just
be,

Exactly where I need to be.

Coming of Age

Is it just a sad fact of life that you will be tired?
It seems like each year passes by without notice,
But each day is felt by the increasing swell of
just pure exhaustion.
Sleep is never beneficial in any quantity,
Sleep too little you feel awful, sleep too much
and you still feel tired,
Sleep the exact amount you are supposed to and
it doesn't feel like enough.
It is a sad constant to have to deal with,
But it is freeing in its own way.
Being tired can no longer become an excuse.
Might as well do what you feel like you need to
do today
Because you're only going to feel tired, if not
more, tomorrow.
Age comes at you fast but it does so as a gift.
You will come to learn exactly what is valuable
to you in this life
By the mere act of what you use with your
ever-dwindling energy.
That beautiful tired feeling in your bones will
only solidify your resolve.

What are we here for?

Life has the meaning you give it,
Or at least that is what I want to think.
But sometimes it feels like meaning is given to
you.
A predisposition to an object, an action, or a
person that you just can't shake loose from your
head.
A nagging desire to sink all your time into
something that makes life worth it for you.
In its own frustrating and exhausting way
A constant demand, a constant feeling of being
drawn toward a future version of yourself
An idolized version that has committed itself
fully to its life's path,
An unwavering strength that you are unable to
be replicated and yet needs to be
That you won't be happy until you've reached
certain heights
Through the fear, the pain, the discomfort
It's terrifying to think maybe it can't work out
and never could
But you just don't know what else to do and so
you must continue on this path
For reasons yourself you can't explain except
that you must.

How to be 26 and Still Living with your Dad.

First off, excluding a crumbling world, you must
fail.
Not to be confused as being a failure, sometimes
it is enough to stay in the game despite the
streak of losing hands being dealt to you.
You must fail at the things that you don't want to
do.
You must fail at the things that you do want to
do.
Pride has to fade and be replaced with humility.
Success has to be changed from its definition
based on those around you and placed within
yourself, a seed of a feeling that must be
nurtured.
You have to trust yourself that the direction your
going is the right way and that it is okay to be
stagnant.
Even time standing still is worth it if you can
watch the sunrise and sunset on your chosen
horizon.
To be 26 and living with your dad is beautiful in
a way,
When you consider when you were young you
never thought you wanted to be 25.

26 has been a good year, an unexpected gift that opened so many possibilities.
Here's to being 27 and living.

Balancing

I try my best to be kind and understanding.
While I think it is important to work hard to be
this way,
I am finding it difficult to maintain.
I think an important part of yourself goes
missing when you constantly put others' feelings
ahead of yours.
Empathy is important but so is a sense of
self-independent from those around you.
It can create a toxic imbalance in a relationship.
Especially once it cannot be sustained anymore,
When you cannot hold back your own emotions
anymore and must speak how you feel,
Others tend to get offended but the sudden shift
in your demeanour.
Unable to reconcile the fact that the person who
makes them feel good about their actions is now
questioning those same actions.
Is it so much to ask to be treated fairly?
I am so tired of bearing everyone's emotional
weight, only to be vilified for my own emotions
when I can no longer carry their burdens.
There is a balance I have yet to figure out, but I
hope one day I do.

The Doorway

I lived most of my life with my foot in the door.
The door that leads to the life I want to lead.
But I was frozen with fear and indecision.
Trying my best to find other ways to reach my
desired destination,
Without ever leaving the doorway,
Afraid to go through it but more afraid it might
shut on me.
What I found was I could never succeed at other
options with my foot planted firmly in the door.
I couldn't open doors to other futures and I
couldn't get any nearer to the one I desired.
It never felt safe to risk either losing the dream
or failing to succeed it.
I've learned now though that I was never going
to get close to succeeding at anything until I
began walking towards it.
So my foot went through that door and the other
one followed.
Now that door lies locked because I shut it.
There is no going back now, the only way I want
to go now is forward.

Fractured

I don't really understand families.
I don't think I ever really have, opting instead to hide away in the closest available basement whenever I was confronted with a family visit.
This only worsened as I grew from a child to a teenager.
As my own close family began to fracture.
A messy break with no hopes to heal properly, family spreading far away like chips of bone swept up in the current of the bloodstream.
There's only so much the bond of blood can hold before it too fades away.
My family interactions began to become less frequent and the family I had seemed to have disappeared one by one over the years.
Now it is just the skeleton crew operating loosely and away from each other.
It is a wound I don't know will ever mend, and I worry it will only be a hindrance when the time comes I must join another family.
I am not sure how to even interact with the concept anymore, I am not sure I ever want to again.
And this is worrying because once what little I have is gone, what will I have left?

Weight Lifting

The brain is pretty incredible for the amount of
weight it can hold.
The body eventually reaches a limit of what it
can hold onto,
The brain can carry something for days, months,
years, even whole lifetimes.
It can be both good and bad depending on what
it carries.
It always seems to be pain that it holds onto the
longest.
Those painful memories that cause you
discomfort,
 It holds onto these until you ache and you lie
awake exhausted.
Going over the scenes again and again.
Trying to find any way it could've gone better
for you or others.
When really the best thing to do for you or
others is to simply let it go.

Best Buds

I am very fortunate to have a group of close
friends.
I wouldn't know how to go through life on my
own.
I know that I wouldn't want to.
But I was lucky enough to find people who
understand me, people I've been able to grow
with over the decades.
We've shared good times, bad times, traumas,
jokes,
We've seen countless jobs and girlfriends and
other friends come and go.
Changing every year like the seasons, but we've
always remained by each other's side.
It is a great blessing to have a constant in the
ever-changing world.
One I do not look over.
I love my friends and my friends love me.
I don't know what my life will look like in the
future, but I know they will be in the picture.

Love

I consider myself to be a romantic.
I am not terribly good at it though.
Love is a tough and ever-changing lesson to
learn, and it is different for each person.
Both in how it is experienced and how it is
shared.
Before I thought love was losing yourself in
another person.
To share in their dreams, interests, and dislikes.
To just be present in their lives and share the
time we have together.
While I think this is a good foundation, just
being there, just being present,
I think there is more to it.
This basic definition made out of lack of
experience doesn't get it right.
It is missing the love you need to give yourself,
first and foremost.
You are not defined by the love you give to
others but by the love you give yourself.
If you don't have this feeling you'll search for it
from others but it cannot and will not ever be
enough.
You do not need to find another half to complete
you, you need to be complete.

And then when you find love it can be
something greater than you ever could've
imagined by yourself.
You are not losing yourself in it, you are not
making yourself whole,
You simply just are in love.
It must be a wonderful place to be.

Progress

It feels like progress is a touchy subject these
days.
The battle for tradition and progress seems to be
a driving force for a lot of issues.
It is difficult to move on because it means
leaving things behind.
No one wants to be left behind and no one wants
what they love to be lost.
But progress is important.
It is what we owe to those whose futures will
extend far beyond our own.
A better place to be than where we found a
home.
If you can't understand where the future is
headed.
Sometimes, it is enough to just not be in the
way.

Youth

There's a saying that youth is wasted on the young.
But I don't think that is correct.
I think it should be that wisdom is wasted on the old.
Youth belongs to the young
The beauty to experience things freely.
To live, to learn, to grow, to watch as the world opens up before your eyes more and more each day.
For those of us who have lived and learned it is difficult to share wisdom with others who have a completely different perspective.
But we need to pass down seeds of ideas with a nurturing and tender hand.
To plant them in others as there is no reason to hold onto them if they can grow no further in us.
It would be a waste to not give it away solely for the fact that the person you gave it to might not water immediately.
It has to be on its own time, you can only hope that it might grow earlier than when you had it.
But sometimes it is enough just to know it will bloom again.

Long Walks

On days when I find my head is too loud
I go on long walks to settle myself down.
I walk until I feel exhausted and then I walk
back from that point.
I find it helps to give yourself perspective.
To think back on how you were so sure you
couldn't do anything but lie in bed,
To look back at the distance you've walked is
encouraging.
As if to prove to yourself,
 I am more capable than I believe myself to be

Diminished

I struggle to accept my own accomplishments.
I don't know why but I can't help but put myself
down instead of offering praise.
I wonder if it's a way to hide.
A way to avoid someone saying a hurtful
comment
Or at least leaning into the blow.
If I don't care it shouldn't hurt when someone
else doesn't.
In reality, it is probably hurting me more.
I think taking away something that makes
someone happy is one of the worst things you
can do.
I am not sure why I do it to myself.

Cry Baby

I struggle to cry.
A remnant of a toxic environment I lived
through.
I found the best way to get by was to not be
noticed
And especially not to be vulnerable.
I have come to a better place in life now, but this
problem remains.
Not out of some prideful rejection of feelings.
But because I find when I truly need to cry and I
feel it about to happen,
I get too excited for the relief it will provide.
To open the floodgates and remove the pressure
building up in your eyes, your throat, your chest.
It causes the moment to pass.
And then I am left waiting for the next moment,
almost eagerly wishing to feel sad again.
This can't be healthy.

Photographs

I've always hated getting photographed.
Maybe it was because it felt like my insecurities
would take shape through the photo.
A piece of evidence confirming all those
negative feelings I've harboured against myself
over the years.
Not liking what I saw, I just avoided them
altogether, whenever possible.
I always just assumed I had no need for them as
I had a keen memory.
I didn't need keepsakes when I thought I'd be
able to call upon the memory whenever I
wished.
That seems to have been a result of the
arrogance of youth.
Brought on by just the sheer lack of lived
experience.
As I grow older and fall further into my vices,
I've realized that memory is not such a
sustainable thing after all.
I regret now not having taken more photos.
I would very much like to go back and look at
my younger self.
Be reminded about who he was through the
choice of fashion and the look in his eyes.

Maybe now I might be able to see beauty where
I used to see flaws.
Maybe now that lost-looking boy might feel
found.

Growth

I've come to realize you do not have to be the
person you have always been.
I used to feel stuck or frozen in the same bad
thoughts, feelings, and situations year after year.
Convinced that was all there was to life.
That everything you did had to be done forever.
Picking one career while you were still
practically a child and having to remain there
until you were of the age to be free from it.
To have to stick to who you were and who you
always had been just because you didn't know
how to be anything else.
A perennial sickness of your character coming
back every year to remind you of the order of
things.
This all seemed better than the alternative of
making yourself vulnerable to change.
A terrifying concept that meant jumping into the
unknown in hopes it would not be as bad as it
was, as it has been.
It seems there was truth to when the adults in
your life told you that you could be anything you
put your mind to.
While this was a comfort as a child it is a
terrifying realization as an adult.

You can be who you want to be.
But it all depends on how hard you are willing to
work for it.
Are you willing to take the jump?

Gratitude

I want to thank you, for taking a moment to be
here with me through these pages.
I have always struggled to express my emotions,
whether out of fear or confusion.
Communication has always been a draining
presence in my life.
Living with the desire, the need to be heard
But not being able to speak up.
I want to thank you for sitting with my thoughts
and feelings over the course of 21 days.
It is my hope that even just one might have been
a comfort, a connection to something, anything.
An expression of who I was as a person,
Even if when I find these pages again I might be
different, you might be different.
At least for this brief time I have been able to
share myself with you.
Even if only for a little while,
I carried all I could.